Waiting in Mindful Hope

WAITING
IN MINDFUL
HOPE

Wisdom for Times of Transition

MARTINA LEHANE SHEEHAN

VERITAS

Published 2016 by Veritas Publications
7–8 Lower Abbey Street
Dublin 1, Ireland
publications@veritas.ie
www.veritas.ie

ISBN 978 1 84730 759 0

10 9 8 7 6 5 4 3 2

The lines from 'Advent' by Patrick Kavanagh are reprinted from
Collected Poems, edited by Antoinette Quinn (Allen Lane, 2004), by
kind permission of the Trustees of the Estate of the late Katherine B.
Kavanagh, through the Jonathan Williams Literary Agency.

A catalogue record for this book is available from the British Library.

Cover designed by Heather Costello, Veritas Publications
Printed in the Republic of Ireland by Anglo Printers, Drogheda

*Veritas books are printed on paper made from the wood pulp of managed forests.
For every tree felled, at least one tree is planted, thereby renewing natural
resources.*

Contents

Introduction

We are a pilgrim people, forever on a journey of transitioning, always waiting in anticipation of the 'not yet'. The Latin word for *Advent* is 'adventus' meaning 'arrival' or 'anticipating the new'. We find ourselves in these *adventus* spaces during every period of transition, whether we are trying to escape a stressful lifestyle, seeking to travel more lightly, or simply listening for what is being created anew.

This book, which can be dipped in and out of, will help you to choose intentional times of awareness, or rather it will help you to notice how awareness is *choosing you*. Initially it was designed as a book specifically for Advent, but as I progressed it became clear to me that this was a book for every season, because the cultivation of *mindful living, attentive waiting* and *hope* are at the cornerstone of authentic living throughout the year.

I hope that this short book will help you to achieve a sense of balance and self-possession, especially during times of stress or change. In striving to get the life for which we yearn, we often neglect the precious in-between times; how often do we find ourselves saying 'once this chapter is over everything will be fine'? What we fail to understand is that it is in the waiting time and transitional spaces that real growth and transformation takes place.

You may be surprised to discover that much of what tires us isn't so much our actual workload, but the constant busyness of our minds. When we begin to integrate present moment attentiveness with compassion and acceptance, we find we are more energetic. By engaging with the suggestions and reflections in this book, you will learn how to break free of that exhausting and incessant mental activity, and learn instead to step into the reality of *the present moment*. In doing so, you will gain a new 'aliveness', but most of all, you will discover that it is in this newly cultivated receptive space that you can become open to 'the more'.

Allow this book to become a companion for transitional and waiting times; allow it to aid you in envisioning new possibilities while attending to what is unfolding in the now. It will help you to find a spiritual steadiness during times of change and help you to surrender to life's vicissitudes; it may even empower you to dance on the shifting sands beneath your feet. It will help you to retain serenity in your life and encourage you to open your heart to the Spirit:

Introduction

May this book guide your heart to know what to leave behind, and what to take with you. May it be a homecoming journey, a return from exile, a discovery of the true self and a rejection of all that is false and illusory. As you lift the lantern of a new hope, may light be cast on your path, may it be done unto you according to the highest plan for your unfolding.

Martina Lehane Sheehan

PART ONE

Waiting

Wakefulness

We have tested and tasted too much, lover —

Through a chink too wide there comes in no wonder.

But here in the Advent-darkened room

Where the dry black bread and the sugarless tea

Of penance will charm back the luxury

Of a child's soul, we'll return to Doom

The knowledge we stole but could not use.

'Advent' by Patrick Kavanagh

Waiting does not come easy to most of us. We live in a world where it is almost fashionable to be stressed from a hectic workload. Society places an increasingly high value on productivity, applauding our ability to multitask and to get work done in record time. Because of this, we can find ourselves being driven to say 'yes' to everyone and everything, even when our inner selves are screaming to say 'no'. While we try to move faster to 'save time' we rarely get to enjoy the time that we have saved. This can come at a high price in terms of our spiritual and psychological well-being. If we are to 'charm back … the child's soul' (which can be another name for 'soul self'), we may have to withdraw a little from our sugar-coated culture of excess in order to appreciate, in Kavanagh's words, 'the newness … in every stale thing'.

WAKEFULNESS

We have to remain aware and awake, St Paul says, because 'the time has come; you must wake up now … the night is almost over, it will be daylight soon' (Rm 13:12). We usually try to console ourselves during waiting times by repeating the mantra that we will: 'be happy when we achieve this goal or reach that particular destination'. When we do this, however, we tune out and so become disconnected from the fertile ground of the present moment. In order to be fully awake, we need to keep vigil and avoid obsessing over the past or the future at the expense of the here and now.

We all have a longing for a less cluttered space in our minds and hearts, and even in our surroundings. It is significant that, in some accounts of his birth, the Creator of the Universe chose a simple cave in which to be born; a cave is an uncluttered, empty space in the centre of the earth, emptied out by the forces of nature. Perhaps, the Spirit also needs this empty space in us, because it cannot fill us if we are already full. Historically, we see that the Good News did not come to the people who were already filled with their own importance, nor was it revealed to those of great power, like Tiberius, Caesar, Pilate or any of the great and powerful. It came instead to people of simplicity, like John the Baptist, who lived an uncluttered and simple life in the wilderness.

The most intrusive clutter usually comes from the chatter in our own heads; that incessant inner dialogue. It is actually the default mode of the mind to envision useless scenarios around *what could be, what should be, what should have happened or what should have been said*. Trapped in these ruminations, our hearts cannot receive the nourishment that is available in the present moment. To be in a *state of receptivity*, we have to *live fully in the present while holding a joyful expectant sense of anticipation of the 'not yet'*. The Advent characters in the first chapter of the Gospel of Luke are not passively waiting. They are waiting intentionally and actively. When we actively wait, we become fully attentive because we trust that something is unfolding moment by moment.

When we are living through times of waiting, we discover that we are not in control; we discover that we cannot change every circumstance by tapping our fingers impatiently on the counter, by honking the horn, or by engaging in some kind of rant. We need, therefore, to learn how to strengthen our ability to wait with patience and mindfulness, instead of considering the waiting period to be a waste of time. 'The farmer waits for the precious crop from the earth, being patient with it until it receives the early and late rains. You also must be patient' (Jas 5:7–8).

Perhaps we could start learning how to wait mindfully in simple ways; when, for example, we are waiting for the kettle to boil or are delayed in a queue in the shop or bank. Here, we can consciously welcome a breathing space, we can look around us and take in sights and sounds and practise being fully present. When velocity and turbulence cause us to tense our shoulders and clench our fists, we can take a breath and choose to let go a little. Instead of filling every spare moment by reaching for our phones to text or access social media, we can practise welcoming times of 'non-doing'. We can do this whenever we find ourselves pounding on the keyboard of computer when a programme will not open fast enough, or repeatedly hitting the button of the pedestrian crossing (imagining we can make the green man appear more quickly). Instead of fuming against these would-be obstacles, we can discover how they are offering an opportunity to strengthen our 'waiting muscles'. All of this helps us towards a more surrendered life, one which helps anxiety to gradually slip away. When we reset our pace and the tempo of our lives, our priorities begin to shift and we begin to align ourselves with Divine Timing.

PATIENT ACCEPTANCE

Instead of feverishly trying to change circumstances, we can bring a gentle acceptance towards whatever is present right now, because no situation (or person) can change until they are first accepted. Anyone who has gone through an addiction recovery programme will endorse the view that the process of acceptance and surrender is a gradual one. Sometimes we have to stay in the stuck places for a while without trying to prematurely 'fix' them. While surrender does not come easy to most of us, it is a crucible for transformation and rebirth. Something can be hatching in the dark that could not otherwise gestate. Nature can help us to creatively embrace the waiting seasons in our souls. Scripture often uses the metaphor of the seed to describe this slow but transformative potential for growth; it tells us that a tiny mustard seed can become the greatest tree where birds come to shelter (cf. Lk 13:18). When the seed is underground and invisible to the eye, it contains all the properties and beauty of the flower. Nature embraces the rhythms of waiting in darkness while lying under the earth. It reminds us of how the Creator of the Universe waited in obscurity and silence before being incarnated into humanity. The Christ Child grew in the womb of a young girl, with no quick fix or grand entry, but a slow and fragile waiting process. This teaches us that the deepest soul movements cannot be rushed, but need to be entered into gently, and patiently inhabited.

In those dark days when we fear we will never see the sun again, when the future is concealed from our sight, we must trust that despite how it seems at present, we are not abandoned. Like the tree in winter which does not yet see the spring, we must feel our rootedness in Divine Soil where eventually we will sense that there are new buds emerging. The transitioning from fear to faith is not easy, but it thaws our frozen hearts and loosens our arthritic spirits.

In times of waiting, we need to be especially aware of how the advertising industry encourages us to find some instant escape route via the attainment of a glitzy new possession or mood-altering substance. It tells us to *bypass waiting times* and instead to catapult ourselves forward into some 'just around the corner' future fantasy. It skilfully works on our 'empty places', convincing us that we do not *have enough*, and of course convinces us that we, ourselves, *are not enough*. This creates the psychological suffering that comes from *craving what we do not have, and rejecting what we do have*. Instead, we can allow ourselves to be encountered *right here, right now* where our parched hearts begin to drink from the tranquil pool of Divine Presence.

A HOLY WASTE OF TIME

We have deep longings for the formless and infinite things of the Spirit; for beauty, love, tenderness, healing and growth. We cannot summon these gifts through willpower alone, but we can *allow* them to unfold and to emerge organically from within. This requires learning how to practise *acceptance and intentional waiting*.

Waiting times are not pointless, but the petulant child within us frequently throws tantrums – lots of them – because of having to wait. We usually want to fix our lives all by ourselves (and of course fix everyone else's also!).

Personally, I don't like to feel directionless, to be without

19

my map or compass. Yet, when looking back on my life I have discovered that these waiting times were the moments when I was most disposed to hear the gentle breeze of the Holy Spirit, where my soul heard 'sshh, be still, I am with you'. It was during these times that I received invitations to release my feverish grasp, to trust that the future will arrive in its own time and to know that I will not receive what I need for tomorrow until tomorrow comes. Instead, I found myself thanking God for the in-between holy 'waste of time'.

SOURCE

In the Gospels we see how Christ, throughout his earthly life, frequently returned to places of solitude, especially in times of major decision-making, as well as before and after his ministry of great teaching and healing. He was frequently to be found communing with his Creator on the hills, out on a lake, in the fields, etc. He knew where his source was; he knew that 'he had come from God and was returning to God' (Jn 13:3). The Temptation of Christ is one such potent example; here, Jesus spent forty days and forty nights in the desert, and refused to be sidelined or seduced into any of the escape routes with which Satan tempted him. Instead he was able to say: 'My kingdom is not of this world' (Jn

18:36). We too are called to discover that our true identity lies in something and somewhere other than the cravings of the false self or the 'kingdoms of this world'. When we taste what the spirit can reveal to us in the silence, nothing else will ever again fully satisfy. This does not mean we reject, or 'bah humbug' the incarnational reality of our lives; far from it in fact. It does mean we no longer look to any created thing to be *our total source of security*. This leads us towards living more joyfully and patiently many of life's unfinished symphonies.

AWAKENINGS

It was a mid-December afternoon, I was impatiently waiting for the lift in a busy department store, my shopping list in hand, in what was a mechanical repetition of every other Christmas excursion. I was on autopilot; cards for those who sent them last year (mentally removing the names of those who didn't send any in return from my list), presents for those who usually gave something in return (while staying within the prescribed price range). Suddenly, I experienced an uncomfortable awakening that stopped me in my tracks. While I did not *hear* a voice, I did *intuit* one, so powerfully that my knees began to weaken and I had to sit down. I bought a cup of coffee and wrote down what I sensed had been communicated to me; it was a simple, uncomplicated question: 'Is there space for me to be born in *your* heart this Christmas?' I felt disturbed, and asked myself what this could mean? I wasn't given any answer, but suffice it to say, the shopping was abandoned and my priorities radically changed for the remaining period coming up to Christmas. Though it is over thirty years ago since that epiphany, it has changed the whole orientation of what the season of Advent – and seasons of waiting – now means for me.

Repentance means to be 'turned upside down'. John the Baptist said 'repent for the kingdom of God is at hand' (Mt 3:2). The Divine Presence can be 'at hand' at times we least expect; any waiting time or place can offer us some kind of personal revelation, because 'we never know the day or hour' (Mt 25:13).

The birth of Christ is not only a historical event, nor reserved only for Christmas or for 'holy people', but something that can take place at any time and in any one of our hearts. Perhaps it might be today that you hear: *Can my breath be your breath? Can my heart be your heart?* In such times your only disposition need be one of 'allowing', your only response need be 'let it be done unto me, according to your word' (Lk 1:38).

Remember:

When you surrender resistance, you recover a lot of your energy and vitality. You need only open your heart to Divine Timing and trust that there is a deeper unfolding, even if it is concealed from your vision right now.

Over to You:

Perhaps you can create an empty space in your home, in a corner of a room. Keep it uncluttered. Allow this place to express your inner places of waiting, or longing. Perhaps reflect on Psalm 62; let it evoke in you some of your heart's longing.

Listening

Waiting need not be a passive activity, where we fundamentally sign away our own power to effect change. Instead, it can be a time when *we intentionally and vigilantly listen* for sight or stirring of the movements of God. We listen in order to respond, so that we can co-create what the Spirit is doing, in us and through us. It is a time to surrender our own fixed idea of *how* and *when* things should happen, because 'with the lord, "a day" can mean a thousand years, and a thousand years is like a day' (2 Pt 8).

Scripture is full of invitations to listen deeply, 'you do not ask for sacrifice and offering but an open ear' (Psalm 39:6). The Book of Isaiah, portrayed like poetry, is filled with the call to wait and to listen: 'Listen, listen to me, and you will have good things to eat and rich foods to enjoy. Pay attention, come to me; listen and your soul will live' (Is 55:2–3).

This type of 'open ear' listening requires us to adjust our antenna. If you are over a certain age, you may remember the old transistor radios in which you had to search for the Radio Luxemburg station. In trying to get a clear signal, you might remember how you had to keep turning the little wheel to avoid the many foreign stations that would frustratingly interfere with your search. Similarly, we have to adjust the antenna of our listening ear, because there are many other 'interfering stations' clamouring for our attention. It is difficult to tune into the still, internal voice amid all these conflicting noises.

AN ATTENTIONAL SHIFT

We can practise this deeper listening each morning when we wake, we can remind ourselves that the next twenty-four hours stretching out before us are brand new, never experienced before. We can approach every person and every task without residual filters from the past or preconceived assumptions about the future. We can practise being fully present when others are speaking, instead of presuming we know what they are going to say next, preparing our own reply or wondering how their story relates to our own! We can, through a simple attentional shift, bring all of ourselves to our simple tasks throughout the day. When, for example, you are washing your hands you can be fully listening to every sound; the gurgle of the water, the breeze or rain outside the window, hearing it all as if for the very first time. In this way all of life becomes a listening, contemplative stance.

We take, on average, twenty thousand breaths each day, and so returning our attention to the breath is a very helpful way of staying fully present in a listening mode. Your breathing doesn't take place in the past or future *but right here and right now*. It can be helpful to locate the place where you connect most deeply with the breath, be it in your chest or in the pit of your stomach. This becomes your anchor, the place towards which you can turn your attention. The Aramaic mantra 'Maranatha' (meaning Come Lord Jesus) is the great listening meditation that can be recited with the rhythm of the breath. It becomes a portal to listening for the sacred in every moment of our day.

BREATHING ANEW

There is a lot of unlearning in the practice of becoming mindful. Like many, I have spent over half of my life in a state of heightened vigilance for what might go wrong next. I learned early in life how to wear out my nerves by trying to make sure nothing could happen that I had not banked on! I learned how to armour myself against any sudden, nasty surprises by making 'clever' vows around self-preservation, so much so, that I smothered all creativity and spontaneity until my poor purple-faced spirit was no longer able to breathe! Learning to live and breathe in an undefended way was not easy because it seemed as if life could break me all over again, but the alternative was spiritual death. It is only when we lose our old life, and our old way of being, that we find a new one (cf. Mt 10:39).

LISTENING ANEW

When, therefore, we become weary, and see no results from our efforts, we need to listen again for the music that may reside beneath the difficulty. We might discover then that the seed of the solution lies hidden in the problem, the medicine in the wound and the resurrection in the death. In the Old Testament, when the Israelites were worn out and despairing, God called them to 'listen carefully to the voice of Yahweh' (Ex 15:26). When our anxiety quietens and we listen more deeply, we will know what to let go of, and what to embrace. We will learn how to *respond to the new, rather than keep reacting to the old*. We discover a great antidote for stress and burnout when we listen, and let go; in fact letting go is the greatest shortcut to well-being.

'We have tested and tasted too much,' Kavanagh observes, suggesting we need to detox with 'dry black bread and sugarless tea' (not very appealing). Times of listening and fasting often go together. John the Baptist, we are told fasted and prayed. Many people fast during the seasons of Advent and Lent. Most of us recoil at even the thought of fasting, yet scripture tells us that there are certain issues that can only be released 'through prayer and fasting' (Mk 9:29). Maybe we could abstain from gulping down our food mindlessly and instead sit gratefully for a few minutes before eating. Many of us are in the habit of ripping open a tin or cardboard covered meal, throwing it in the microwave and onto a plate to wolf it down while texting or watching television. In a life pumped by adrenaline, noise and speed, we eat heartily whenever the opportunity arises, but how often do we really taste or savour what we're consuming? Have we lost a sense of gratitude for the banquet of being alive? When we listen more deeply, we might discover that it is our anger that we are eating, or perhaps eating our anxiety, or even binging out of sheer boredom. Genuine fasting is not some kind of punitive act undertaken for the sake of being miserable, but something that can actually lead us to a more authentic abundance, where we begin to really taste and see that life is good.

TASTING ANEW

Something as simple as spending more time enjoying meals can turn ordinary rituals into little sacred ceremonies. We are then more likely to wait until we are hungry before eating, and more likely to eat with reverence. If, for example, you are about to scoff down a packet of chocolate biscuits, try waiting for a few moments and you may discover that it is *your mind* that is craving the chocolate *and not your body*. You will find that those few minutes of waiting and listening allow you to pay attention to your many dislocated longings for food and so you begin *to choose* whether you want to eat or not. Or at least you can choose not to scoff the entire packet!

Maybe we have old conditioned beliefs about life not being for enjoyment, so we sneak a moment's pleasure (in case there might not be enough left over). We gobble it up as quickly as possible, hoping that nobody notices, or hoping that we ourselves don't notice (before our internal critic kicks in, and kicks us). When we have learned from a young age to amputate all delight from our lives, we end up trying to steal a little pleasure when we can, while pretending we didn't really enjoy it! Accustomed to finding escape hatches from being human through some kind of false frugality, we confuse simplicity with self-stinginess.

Shopping – especially coming up to Christmas – is full of 'temptations' and our willpower tends to falter. Shelves are lined with chocolates, especially near the cash register where you cannot avoid them, while you wait in line. Instead of following the compulsion to get high on artificial stimulants, you can take a breath and a listening pause and allow a deeper connection with the *real inner hunger*. That simple acknowledgement will help you make a more mindful choice and keep you connected to your heart's deepest longings.

We do not have to focus only on food where fasting is concerned; perhaps we could fast from constantly listening to bad news, or from excessive reliance on television or from continually checking screens, be it to access email or social media. When we do this, we create space for a new direction, a new path; scripture calls us to 'Prepare a way for the Lord, make his paths straight' (Mk 1:3).

We can clear away new paths by fasting from words that do not bless ourselves or others; maybe we could deliberately create a gossip-free zone in our homes! While we might initially miss hearing the latest instalment of juicy gossip, we will eventually feel the reward of a lighter heart.

There is a notice on the wall at reception in our retreat house that contains a message many of you will be familiar with:

Waiting in Mindful Hope

Before you add something to a conversation, ask yourself if what you are about to say can pass through these three gates:

1. Is it kind?
2. Is it necessary?
3. Is it true?

I tried asking myself the three questions before reacting to a politician that I have a particular aversion towards. Each time he appears on television, I try to become aware, and so refrain from my usual rant, and while it hasn't changed him, it has made me less reactive. (Well, just a tiny bit …)

Through awareness, we begin to be less critical and more compassionate. There is an old mindfulness meditation exercise called 'Loving Kindness' which involves sending blessings to people (including yourself). You can say something like 'may you be happy, may you be well'. Start with your own name and then extend it to others (including those you may have difficulty with). There is a beautiful old Irish blessing called St Patrick's Breastplate, reproduced overleaf, which can be said/sung each day.

Saint Patrick's Breastplate

I arise today
Through a mighty strength, the invocation of the
Trinity,
Through belief in the Threeness,
Through confession of the Oneness
of the Creator of creation.
I arise today
Through the strength of Christ's birth with His
baptism,
Through the strength of His crucifixion with His
burial,
Through the strength of His resurrection with His
ascension,
Through the strength of His descent for the judgment
of doom.
I arise today
Through the strength of the love of cherubim,
In the obedience of angels,
In the service of archangels,
In the hope of resurrection to meet with reward,
In the prayers of patriarchs,
In the predictions of prophets,
In the preaching of apostles,

Waiting in Mindful Hope

In the faith of confessors,
In the innocence of holy virgins,
In the deeds of righteous men.
I arise today, through
The strength of heaven,
The light of the sun,
The radiance of the moon,
The splendor of fire,
The speed of lightning,
The swiftness of wind,
The depth of the sea,
The stability of the earth,
The firmness of rock.
I arise today, through
God's strength to pilot me,
God's might to uphold me,
God's wisdom to guide me,
God's eye to look before me,
God's ear to hear me,
God's word to speak for me,
God's hand to guard me,
God's shield to protect me,
God's host to save me
From snares of devils,
From temptation of vices,

From everyone who shall wish me ill,
afar and near.
I summon today
All these powers between me and those evils,
Against every cruel and merciless power
that may oppose my body and soul,
Against incantations of false prophets,
Against black laws of pagandom,
Against false laws of heretics,
Against craft of idolatry,
Against spells of witches and smiths and wizards,
Against every knowledge that corrupts man's body
and soul;
Christ to shield me today
Against poison, against burning,
Against drowning, against wounding,
So that there may come to me an abundance of
reward.
Christ with me,
Christ before me,
Christ behind me,
Christ in me,
Christ beneath me,
Christ above me,
Christ on my right,

Waiting in Mindful Hope

Christ on my left,
Christ when I lie down,
Christ when I sit down,
Christ when I arise,
Christ in the heart of every man who thinks of me,
Christ in the mouth of everyone who speaks of me,
Christ in every eye that sees me,
Christ in every ear that hears me.
I arise today
Through a mighty strength, the invocation of the
Trinity,
Through belief in the Threeness,
Through confession of the Oneness
of the Creator of creation.

Remember:

When we listen more deeply, we will know what to let go of, and what to embrace.

Over to You:

Concentrate on really listening today. Maybe begin with the prayer, 'Speak Lord your servant is listening' (Is 46:3–4). Listen to all the sounds that you never really hear on a busy day. Before you indulge in food today, listen and attend to the deeper hunger. When you are in conversation, choose to intentionally listen to how you are being blessed through this person, this situation.

Discernment

Taking time for discernment is, in many ways, a countercultural practice, especially since society places such a high value on our being in charge of our own destiny and on our always having a contingency plan. Some people think discernment is simply deciding between two options, a choice between Plan A or Plan B. The process of discernment is rarely that simple, nor is it a choice between good and bad; it is, instead, about attending to the 'neutral zone' or transitional place. This is something we usually recoil from, because here neither the past nor the future are entirely in our grasp and we can feel trapped in a liminal – or 'inbetween' – state.

Apparently, in the cocoon stage before the caterpillar becomes a butterfly it has to go through a stage of being 'nothing'– neither a caterpillar or a butterfly. This metamorphosis is similar for us, we often enter a stage that feels like a dark night; when our very identity is dismantled but we know we cannot go back to the old life. Here, we can only ground ourselves by taking small steps, one at a time, until we are lead safely across the bridge of transition. We often feel adrift when something of our old life has changed, when a role or a job has ended, and so we have to affirm that our true essence is deeper than all of the roles that we play in life. It is here that we find ourselves having to discern where we are being led, we have to *wait in hope*, trusting that this dark phase will give way to something new, 'you will have pain, but your pain will turn into joy' (Jn 16:20). Gradually we have to trust that we will receive *inner serenity in exchange for outer security*.

The plant outside my window is pouring out of its pot; it is screaming for a bigger holding place. It reminds me of the many times I have had to be repotted. Rarely have I chosen it, but life has frequently shown me when I need new soil and a bigger pot. 'Who am I now?' I protest without my familiar securities. 'You are a child of the universe,' the old poem says, 'no less that the trees and the stars – you have a right to be here' ('Desiderata').

NEW BOOTS

'Be careful that you don't get too big for your boots,' an English teacher continually warned us in school. But maybe we *do need* to outgrow old boots, maybe we need to get more spacious ones, especially when we are developing corns from the old ones!

Sometimes a personal metamorphosis is not of our choosing and can feel more like an earthquake in our inner landscape. We may feel displaced and while we are, for all intents and purposes, still alive and breathing, we can feel shattered inside. Too paralysed to move from the old and still no sight of the new, we have to turn inward and discern the promptings that lead us forward. The great teacher of discernment, Ignatius of Loyola, advises us to ask God for what we desire, but reminds us that we have *a pull and counter pull* where these desires are concerned. In other words, we have both resistance and attraction to what is truly life-giving; our deepest self has a desire for growth and freedom, while the false self clings to things like *control and rigidity*. We discover then that we are at a knife edge because what serves our ego is usually at variance with the longings of our inner selves. We have, according to the father of psychoanalysis Sigmund Freud, a *life instinct and death instinct* operating in us. Scripture tells us that sometimes we even prefer darkness to light (cf. Jn 3:19). Of course we have to respect the full array of complex human desires, each clamouring for our attention; however, while we may have to allow them to have their say, we need not be ambushed by them.

The deepest desire in our hearts is the one that is most congruent with God's desire, in fact, it is Divinely planted in us. Perhaps we could say that our spiritual journey is all about desire; God desired us into existence and our deepest desire is to experience our oneness with our God. We may have to discard old cramped boots and embrace bigger and more spacious ones as we expand into all that we can be.

THE GENTLE VOICE

Many people find the Old Testament story of Elijah to be helpful in times of discernment. Here, Elijah encounters God in the gentle breeze (cf. 1 Kgs 19:11–13). It wasn't in the clamouring sounds of hurricane, earthquake, or fire; it was only when these sounds passed by that he heard the gentle breeze from which Yahew spoke. Initially, Elijah reacted to each of these passing sounds. Likewise, with us; we often jump in reaction to the compulsive, volcanic thought patterns in our minds. Inner landscapes can shift like tectonic plates on the earth's crust, especially when we become distressed by our own internal chatter which can be so full of 'heat'. Instead, we can learn to discern how we have allowed ourselves to become imprisoned by our own reactions to the aberrations of others, and how we can often keep those reactions alive for a whole day, or maybe even a whole lifetime. Even though the universe may be offering us consolation, we sometimes stay in the shadowed desolation of our own internal dark mood.

How do we know *what to let pass through our minds and what to take on board?* Firstly, we can recognise that the Spirit rarely manifests in a loud or forceful manner, but comes silently and subtly. Many people say the presence of the Spirit brings a feeling of 'homecoming', it feels congruent with some deeply held life value, or as we frequently say 'it brings consolation'. Therefore, even though God's call can be challenging, something in us recognises it as a homecoming. Maybe the very situation that you are desperately trying to *run away from* is actually the one in which God is *running towards you*. Maybe the self you are trying to flee from is the one that Christ happily resides in. Maybe it is when we stop obstructing the view that we recognise the guidance of the outstretched hand.

GUIDANCE

Scripture uses the metaphor of sheep and shepherd to describe the discernment of the voice that brings security and belonging (Jn 10:1–21). It tells us that the shepherd 'knows and has concern for', in contrast to the thief 'who has no regard'. As part of our discernment process, we can begin to ask *whose voice am I following here? Is it the bringer of life, or the thief? Is it society's voice, or my own 'superego'* (Freud's term for one's inner critic)? *Is it the voice of my ego or the voice of my real self?* Thomas Merton says that the ego self is that which believes it has total autonomy through power and control. The true self, in contrast, lives in communion with God and others.

The prophet Isaiah tells us that God is a teacher, 'I, Yahew, your God, teach you what is good for you, I lead you in the way that you must go' (Is 48:17). We are even told that there is a recognisable joy and peace when we follow the guidance of this teacher: 'your happiness would be like a river, your integrity like the waves of the sea' (Is 48:18).

One of the recommended ways we retain strength and consolation through times of discernment is through savouring again the *remembrance of God's presence through former times of change.* We can consciously recall how God has been with us, loving us and supporting us in the past, 'whom I have carried since the womb, whom I have supported since you were conceived' (Is 46:3–4). This is a powerful message in terms of our being able to trust that God is with us in the 'in-between' times. We are assured that, just as we were accompanied in the past, we will continue to be so in the future, 'until your old age I shall be the same, until your hair is grey I shall carry you' (Is 46:4). Releasing the past with gratitude and welcoming the future with faith allows us to live and savour the present more fully.

SAVOURING CONSOLATION

We need to savour the experience/touch of God's love in an embodied, incarnational way. This furnishes us with the ability to trust that we are, we have been, and we always will be loved and guided.

Sarah was sifting through the gifts which she had received for her First Communion, she was laying them out on the table and looking at them again. 'What did you enjoy best about the day?' I asked her. She thought for a moment, grinned up at me, proudly displaying her gapped teeth and chirply said, 'What I enjoyed most of all was that *it was all about me.*' Then she gave a little twirl, relishing her beautiful dress. '*All about me*: hmm, that sounds familiar,' I said to myself, and before I could start to analyse what the implications of that might be, she went on to explain further: 'I enjoyed seeing my aunt come home from England, my granny arriving this morning, the photos, the pictures …' Her eyes were alight as she recalled everything that was beautiful about the day. Sarah was 'treasuring all these things in her heart', making them her own, absorbing every detail – the feel of her new Communion shoes, the look in the eyes of those celebrating

45

her. Eventually, she got sleepy and as she began to doze off, she asked her dad to recount all the day's events for her once again.

Sarah reminds us of a very important part of our discernment process – *the need to receive and absorb moments of consolation, which can then sustain us in times of desolation.* How does the tender fragile rose open up in all its beauty? Only because it receives and absorbs the warmth and light of the sun. Likewise for us, we have to savour the light and the warmth of Divine consolation – so much so, that we can allow it to shine back out into the world.

Remember:

The situation you may be trying to run away from could be the very one in which God may be running towards you. Maybe the self you are trying to flee from is the one where Christ happily makes his home.

Over to You:

Identify a crossroads in your life at this time; sketch the various options. Pray the words 'Yahew, make your ways known to me, teach me your paths' (Ps 25:4). Name and write what feels like your deepest desire at this time, take one step towards this choice, while paying close attention to how it feels in the body.

PART TWO

Mindfulness

Coming to Our Senses

Mindfulness essentially means 'lucid awareness'. Many people think it is a new phenomenon, but in truth mindfulness is an ancient practice. 'Watchfulness' was a term used to describe a practice espoused by the desert fathers and mothers in the third and fourth century AD. It has echoes of what today we call 'mindfulness'. These nomads were known for their lives of simplicity, solitude, hospitality and they lived counter-culturally on the margins. They practised watchfulness, not as a mechanical technique but as a conscious intention towards surrendering to God's presence.

Today, we are excavating the lessons on how to live more mindfully, instead of incessantly dwelling on the past or thinking about the future. We can do this, not by avoiding ruminative thoughts, but by discovering that we do not have to give them the full stage, or our full consent. When we look at thoughts objectively we see them for what they are – just thoughts – and, as such, we find we no longer react to their emotional charge; instead we create a spaciousness around them. We are then more able to step back from the mind's default mode with its many seductive and often vicious mental spirals. Because neurological pathways are created through habits, each time we repeat a particular habit, the pathway gets embedded; however, through regular meditative practice and determined awareness, we can learn how to withdraw from these habitual trails. We may well find that this reduces the recurrence of anxiety and depression. Likewise, with physical pain, if we create a relationship with *the pain itself*, rather than many reactionary thoughts *about* the pain, we reduce a lot of our afflictive emotions.

A simple returning of our awareness to the breath helps us to connect with the natural self, where we discover a renewed attentiveness and vitality. It also empowers us to exercise more choice around our responses to daily events. We discover a more panoramic view of our lives, instead of fixating on every problem at hand.

YOU ARE NOT YOUR THOUGHTS

Whenever we have a negative or unresourceful thought, it will lead to a distressing feeling and consequently, to an uncomfortable body sensation. For example, if your internal voice repeats phrases such as 'I'm not good enough' or 'I am not confident', the muscles in the body react by tightening or tensing. This in turn affects our behaviour, and so, for instance, you might start to avoid certain social events or situations that begin to feel 'threatening'. When you become aware that you are 'buying into' these thoughts, you recognise that *you have a choice*. Instead of allowing the stories in your mind to determine your feelings and actions, you can ask yourself *what one positive step can I take right now?* You then begin to move in the direction of your goals and values, rather than being at the mercy of a conglomeration of critical or fearful thoughts.

Whenever you notice your mind whirring in distressing circles, instead of engaging in the details, gently label this activity as 'thinking' or 'worrying', and you will become aware that *you are not your thoughts*. Unfortunately, what we usually do in such situations is start to battle with the thoughts, which, of course, makes us even more agitated. Furthermore, when we are embroiled in an inner battle, we are not able to concentrate on anything other than what is bothering us.

Soon after my wedding, I went to visit an elderly relative, to introduce her to Pat, my husband. After he greeted her, she continued to grip his hand, and leaned ever further towards his face while staring at him intently. I thought to myself how lovely it was that she was so interested in getting to know him. She then blurted out, without a moment's hesitation, 'Are they your own teeth?

Later I found out that she had just received her new dentures and was in great discomfort trying to get used to them, and so whenever she met someone she saw only their teeth!

When we are in physical or emotional discomfort, we often become so embroiled in it that we cannot be present to anything except what is bothering us. However, when, with compassion and acceptance, we turn towards and greet what is bothering us, it tends to dissolve. Paradoxically, when we acknowledge the discomfort, we are no longer obsessed with it and so can bring attention back to the person or situation that we are engaged with at that moment.

THE PRESENCE MOMENT

We can cultivate a way of being present to the moment – and, as I like to add, 'to *the presence* in the moment'! While a lot of contemporary mindfulness literature is underpinned by Buddhist philosophy, there is a strong Christian mindfulness tradition that is perhaps less well known. Many contemplatives, such as Teresa of Ávila, John of the Cross, Catherine of Siena and Thomas Merton, have written extensively on the concept of having an inner cell, a place of stillness and silence. They suggested (in the language of their time) that when we descend into our truest selves, we discover God at the heart of our being. The Spanish mystic John of the Cross discovered that we have to descend to the inner empty space. He writes:

> To come to enjoy all,
> Desire joy in nothing;
> To come to possess all,
> Desire to possess nothing.

Perhaps he is saying that when we let go of some of our 'possessiveness', we discover that we already 'possess all'. We discover then that *we have enough* and *we are enough*. The mystic adds 'to come to that which you do not know, you must go on a path you do not know'. The path 'we do not know' disposes us to live with what the Buddhists call 'a beginner's mind'. This means that instead of allowing the stale stories or conversations of yesterday to invade today, we begin anew to see everyone and everything as if for the very first time. How wonderful and alive we would be if this were so.

'Apatheia', a word which comes from the early desert tradition, refers to a state of non-reactivity or detachment. John Cassian, a monk who lived from AD 360 to 435, travelled in the desert of Palestine and Egypt, recording desert wisdom. He advised cultivating a spirit of *apatheia* through 'interior work' and suggests we:

1. Renounce attachment to passing thoughts;
2. Let go our over-adherence to fixed mental images of God;
3. Reduce whatever in our lives brings anxiety, disharmony or idolatry.

The desert dwellers were speaking in the language of their day; nowadays we do not refer to such things as 'idolatry states', but instead we refer to 'ego states'. Cultivating a spirit of *apatheia* does not mean we dispassionately numb ourselves from a full engagement with life, nor should we develop some kind of fixed witnessing observation, but we can disengage from our ego's needy cravings. Defending our ego is exhausting because it is driven by our inner insecurity; therefore, we give ourselves a huge health boost by releasing our attachment to ego defences.

Finally, living simply in the moment necessitates that we pare back our belongings a little, and when we do, we will notice the abundance in everything we *already have* (rather than continuously craving what we do not have). When we live simply, we discover the essentials, and so we allow what is most true and most beautiful to come to the surface. We will find ourselves beginning to live with more gratitude, an essential ingredient for happiness.

Remember:

A distressing thought leads to a distressing feeling and a distressing body sensation. You can choose your thoughts! You can choose to believe that you have enough and you are enough.

Over to You:

Choose something you do several times a day, for example, washing the dishes or taking the dog for a walk; bring full awareness to the task at hand, engaging all of your senses. Instead of seeing everything as just something to be 'got over', see each of them as a sacred activity. Look around your home, see everything as if for the first time, while releasing any possessiveness. This may even lead to a desire to give some things away.

Heartfulness

While the research findings in favour of practising mindfulness are very impressive, there is a danger we will approach meditation with a consumerist mentality; focusing on what *we can gain*. We might show up for prayer only for the goodies, 'give me my inheritance, my allotted portion of relaxation and wholeness,' we say to God. This can be like arranging to meet a friend for dinner where we are only really interested in the dinner, and not the friend!

'In the morning, long before dawn, he got up and left the house and went to the lonely place and prayed there' (Mk 1:35). These are my favourite lines in scripture; there is something alluring about this person of Christ sneaking away for repose during the busiest times of his life, often after a period of time preaching and healing. He went there, not for personal gain per se but to tune into his connection with the Creator. This attunement became his very breath, the music behind everything he did, and everything he was. Clearly, he didn't seek his identity from the approval of others, nor was he too worried about handing out evaluation forms! Instead, his deepest vision and identity came from the stillness. The contemplative dimension seemed to be at the cornerstone of his ministry. Perhaps it was because of his commitment to 'the lonely place' that he espoused that unique luminosity, an inner authority that we are told was different to that of the scribes and Pharisees (cf. Mk 1:22). Jesus was quite clear about where his power came from, 'it is the Father living in me who is doing this work' (Jn 14:10). This gave him a clarity about the 'why' of his mission: 'My food to do the will of the father' (Jn 4:34).

Without a solitary place we lose anchorage, we become dependent on externals for our identity, where we often try to become all things to all people. When we find ourselves rebounding from highs of self-importance to lows of self-loathing (which are opposite sides of the same coin), we are trapped in a prison of our own making. For example, we might be surprised to discover how much of what we do is motivated by our own need for some kind of validation, one that might give us a semblance of self-worth. In begging for scraps of approval, we often turn our work and achievements into little gods that we worship but which leech the very life out of our souls. Usually, it is only when we grow tired of our many failed recipes (for a perfect self) and weary of continually trashing ourselves that we willingly crawl onto the rock where we can rest. Despite the swirling storms within and without, on this rock, we can rest and yield to the love that is enfolding us (without any striving on our behalf).

DESERT CALL

Many people find themselves longing to withdraw for a few hours or days or even months of stillness. In our retreat house, people often book in for a day of silence; a 'desert day'.

The desert appears frequently in scripture as a place for listening and discernment. The prophet Hosea was told by God that Israel would be led to the desert, where God would speak: 'that is why I am going to lure her and lead her out into the wilderness and speak to her heart' (Hos 2:16). In the New Testament, John the Baptist went out into the desert, where he wore camel clothing and ate locusts and wild honey. Jesus, at the beginning of his ministry, went into the desert – to a dry, arid, silent place. Desert spirituality was revived and systemised in the early 1970s by the Cistercian monk, Thomas Keating. His meditative practice is known as 'Centering Prayer'. Around the same time, the Benedictine monk John Main, teacher of 'Christian Meditation', set up a meditation centre in Ealing Abbey in West London. Both Keating and Main emphasised a similar meditative practice, one that is not dependent on thoughts, feelings or images. This challenges our western habit of placing such a very high value on an intellectual and conceptual approach to understanding the Divine and neglecting the practice of 'experiencing' God, in a sensory, moment-by-moment way.

While most meditation practices have emphasis on breath, and on the dis-identification with passing thoughts, etc., prayer is intrinsically relational; it is about union and communion with the Trinity. We cannot fall in love with a technique or a practice, we can only truly *find ourselves, and let go of ourselves in a relationship of love.*

Divine Presence is both immanent and transcendent, and is so awesome to human comprehension that we are told that 'no one can see the face of God and live' (Ex 33:20). So much so that Moses fainted when he encountered the Divine! Contemplative practice does not end in a trinity of 'me, myself and I'! A client once said to me, after we had completed a long, therapeutic counselling journey, 'Now that I have *received* myself, I feel ready to *let go* of myself.' Something in us also knows that we are made to let go of ourselves because we are created to be part of the great Trinitarian love story, which weaves together the search for the God who is within us, yet beyond us. Something deep in us knows that nothing else will fully satisfy, and so we cannot settle for some vague, spiritual energies devoid of flesh and blood. Pope Francis cautions us to 'see the growing attraction to various forms of a "spirituality of well-being" divorced from any community life, or to a "theology of prosperity" detached from responsibility for our brothers and sisters.'

Mindfulness, should not in itself (in my opinion), become a *replacement* for prayer, instead we can see it as *preparing the way* (an apt theme for Advent). The practice of becoming mindful can prepare us to *intentionally dedicate and orientate ourselves to resting and listening to the One who gazes on us with delight*.

I have to admit that I don't always desire prayer, in fact sometimes I will do anything (even housework, some would be surprised to hear) rather than sit in stillness. However, I know my soul needs it as much as my body needs oxygen. Prayer, for me, is a burrowing down to a place beneath my jumpy, unreliable surface self; it is not about thinking, but resting. It is about leaving behind my to-do lists and self-help kits and entering into the inner room. Sometimes, I go there dragging my feet and full of restlessness. Sometimes my spiritual 'sweet tooth' is craving something more exciting – a few heavenly visions or maybe even levitation! However, I have learned that it is better not to move the goalposts according to my mood, but just to show up and shut up! I need to do this, not just sporadically, but each day, regardless of my emotional temperature and whether it is sun, rain or clouds that greet me. 'What's the point, if you don't *feel* anything during prayer?' a friend asked me recently. That question made me search for the fruits, if any, of my commitment to the inner cell. I suppose what I most clearly notice is the subtle but continuous dismantling of the ego self (the part that's always racing ahead towards the next bigger and better goal or ambition). Perhaps I am also less buffeted about by the changing circumstances and opinions of everyone around me. However these 'benefits' fade into oblivion when I reflect on the sweet relief that comes with knowing that I am loved without limits and so don't have to overcome or weed out all my imperfections. I only have to lean into the love that disentangles the knots created by my ill-advised attempts at self-salvation.

Remember:

You do not have to perfect yourself, you need only intentionally lean into the love that sustains and transforms you.

Over to You:

Try to introduce a practice of pausing and reflecting first thing in the morning. You will resist it initially, but you will find that there is a special numinous quality about morning time. Just show up, and if you do not know how to pray, allow silence to do its work, allow the Spirit to pray in you (cf. Rm 8:26).

A Way of Life

'Take the cell with you,' the desert dwellers advised. 'Pray constantly,' we are told in scripture (1 Th 5:16–18). Perhaps we can see these as invitations to revert to a rhythmic practice of returning to awareness whenever we get caught in habitual anxiety. Like slowly released nutrients, we then gradually experience a little more peace and begin to move with a little less haste. When you find your home in the cell of stillness, you can 'carry your home' anywhere. 'Homecoming' is a state, not a place. It is a sitting into one's own truth, and a more comfortable wearing of one's own skin. Otherwise, we may find ourselves crowing about our qualifications, or our possessions; and of course, others yell back even louder and nobody is actually heard. When we know who we are, there is no more need to yell, because *we are already home, and already heard*, even in our silence.

If we really know that we are blessed and beloved, we would much more easily be able to let go of the petty stuff and the slights to our good name would not sting so much.

How wonderful it would be to be that free. Maybe we can 'fake it, till we make it'! Breathing out, we can say 'I am letting go'; breathing in we can say 'I am home'. Try it and see if the rhythmic surrender calms you a little, especially when you find yourself fuming at those who are not in accord with you, or at those who keep challenging your patience.

You can begin to make small (or not so small) changes in your day. For example, in the morning, instead of putting on the radio, or checking your phone, pay attention to each task, whether it is making a cup of tea, tying your shoe laces or brushing your teeth. Just be in the moment, and 'come to your senses', rather than catastrophising the day before it even starts.

Remember that all those morning ruminations – the 'what if' and 'ah, but' scenarios in your head – will create 'what if' and 'ah, but' realities in the day ahead! Only the now is real – the rest is illusion. Even a few moments of pausing will help you access the clarity to handle whatever arises in the day ahead.

Throughout the day, we can begin to cultivate a practice whereby when we are walking, we are just walking, one step at a time, thus removing the focus from our wish to be somewhere else. When we are fully there, life enters into us and becomes a source of spiritual strength.

BREATH

Memories of my mother's final weeks are filled with rasping and gasping as she longed desperately for what none of us could give her – the gift of breath. Her eyes looked pleadingly into ours, bewildered that we could not rescue her from a shortage of air, the deprivation of her next inward breath. Even now I can still hear the gasping sounds; it stops me in my tracks and reminds me to give thanks for this gift of respiration.

In the Old Testament, the Hebrews had a deep reverence for the gift of breath – they saw it as God's way of sharing the Divine Life with them. In the New Testament, we are told Jesus *breathed* on the Apostles in sending them the Holy Spirit.

We are all breathing the same air, the same oxygen that renews our cells. 'May they all be one' was the dream of Jesus (Jn 17:21). We can easily lose sight of that 'oneness' and become divided from ourselves, from one another and from nature. Human beings often assume superiority, seeing themselves as the pinnacle of creation. However, anyone who carries an inner silence gradually becomes more sensitive to the natural world. It is paradoxical to hold a contemplative stance while exploiting nature or animals. In the scriptures we are told that if one member suffers, all of the body suffers (cf. 1 Cor 12:6–18). We are part of the breath of a delicately balanced ecosystem. We are asked to 'Stay awake, praying at all times' (Lk 21:36). Staying awake allows our respiration to be in unison with the breath of the whole universe. Pope Francis, in his groundbreaking encyclical *Laudato Si'*, writes:

> Everything is related and we human beings are united as brothers and sisters on a wonderful pilgrimage, woven together by the love God has for each of his creatures and which also unites us in fond affection with brother sea, sister moon, brother river and mother earth.

Abba Joseph of the desert fathers advised, 'If you want to find rest here and hereafter, say on every occasion, "Who am I?" and do not judge anyone.' It is human nature to complain bitterly about the person who has offended us; however, although we get temporary relief we usually feel worse afterwards. If instead we were to ask ourselves 'Who am I?', and ask it several times until it penetrates to the core, we might choose a different route. We would touch the place where we are all one and more similar than we realise, we would seek healing rather than hurting, and so find more 'rest here and hereafter'.

Remember:

Try not to hold on too tightly to the 'nice moments', or contract against the difficult ones. Instead, bring a gentle acceptance towards it all, softening a little towards life's complexities.

Over to You:

Deliberately leave spaces in your schedules, allow for 'interruptions'; they may be life's surprises arranged for you by providence. If you find yourself being aggressively reactive to somebody, ask yourself 'Who am I?' Maybe write the question down and allow a response to emerge.

PART THREE

Hope

Acceptance

It is 6 a.m. and the boisterous crows are lined up on the roof of the house like a rock band during pre-concert rehearsal. They are looking at me, heads tilted as if to say, 'so what are you going to do about us?' I am annoyed with them and annoyed with myself for being annoyed, thus ensuring I am creating another lousy morning for myself. The weeds have grown up through the gravel again from last week's rain, and oh no, there is dog poo on the footpath – blast it, blast her! I start to hug my little irritations close to me, weaving them around my heart until I am a bundle of irritation. If only those crows would shut up; if only I could finally beat those weeds; if only she would do her business somewhere else. If only …

Then I see the hill behind our house; it looks different every day; this morning, it is striped with the interplay of sun and shadow. Suddenly, it dawns on me that life is striped with sun and shadow. I am constantly trying to make it one or the other even though it was never all sun or all shadow, and it never will be. I too am striped with sun and shadow; one moment

I want to feed the world and save the rainforests, the next I want to assassinate the crows, the dog and whoever comes near me! Acceptance eventually dissolves my irritation and I begin to feel a little more tranquil, in a stripy kind of way. I might even begin to bless this mess: the crows, the weeds and even the dog poo!

Buddhists tell us that we create suffering for ourselves through non acceptance of life *as it is*. We create frustration for ourselves whenever we have too many fixed outcomes attached to our hopes. When, for example, you hold inflexible expectations about how life *should be*, how others *should be*, you are bound to become disappointed. We don't just try to change situations, we also try to *change people* in some subtle (but slightly superior) way. Admit it, you know how it goes: we say 'I am only saying this now for your own good', but we are really saying 'please become more like who *I want you to be*'.

OPENNESS

The Jewish people had 'fixed expectations'. They expected the Messiah to come in a warlike guise; they hoped for a God who would fight their battles for them, who would be exclusively on their side. Gradually, over time, a more compassionate God came into consciousness. The Book of the Prophet Isaiah is filled with hopeful anticipation for a

God of tenderness, a God who would console and heal. This is our journey also – we too have to evolve from closed and rigid expectations to ones that are open and fluid. Hope does not change difficult circumstances but it *changes our relationship* to those difficult situations. Instead of harbouring those many subtle 'pouts' when things do not *go our way*, we can say, *let it be done unto me according to your word, according to your time, according to your plan for me*. Hope, therefore, is not a list of wants and entitlements, but more of an enlivening openness to possibility which can move through us and fill the empty corners of our hearts. We can wait in mindful hope because we know that the Holy Spirit will guide us according to our readiness, because 'some of the answers might be too much for us now' (Jn 16:12).

Hope is a prominent theme in Advent, 'hold your head high, your liberation is close at hand' (Lk 21:28). To have eyes of hope is to look for the miracle of new growth in the most barren of circumstances and to wait for the flicker of light when we walk through valleys of darkness. We long for a world where 'the blind see again, and the lame walk, lepers are cleansed, and the deaf hear, and the dead are raised to life and the Good News is proclaimed to the poor' (Mt 11:5). We need to ask ourselves what part of us has become lame or what lame excuses might be holding us back? We need to continually ask for a restoring of our spiritual sight.

BEARERS OF HOPE

We are not meant to be passive spectators where the world's suffering is concerned; instead, we must be bearers of hope, communicating to others that all is not lost, that the dawn follows the darkness. Pope Francis says:

> each day in our world beauty is born anew, it rises transformed through the storms of history. Values always tend to reappear under new guises, and human beings have arisen time after time from situations that seemed doomed.

We are to be people of hope, 'anointed to bring the good news to the poor' (Luke 4:18). Where are the poor around us, and where is our sphere of influence?

HOPE IN PLACES OF EXILE

Scripture is full of promises of hope for those in exile. The Hebrew scriptures portray a group of people crying out for a saviour to deliver them. The prophet Isaiah spoke to those who were returning home after years of exile. Just as they were beginning to get used to being in the desert, they were unsettled again and told to go back home; however, they were assured that God would be with them during this transitional time (Is 35:4). They were told that their dignity would be restored, they would rediscover their true identity and would become like 'precious jewels in the hand of their God' (Is 62:3). When we understand the yearnings of these ancient people, we understand too the great suffering of those who are in exile today; the many refugees who are longing for homeland. We also shed light on our own places of exile, whether psychological, emotional or spiritual. There are parts of ourselves that have been sent into exile, the parts that have been split off, repressed or deemed 'not good enough' (usually by ourselves). There are parts of us that have never been invited into the light, but instead have been assigned to the hidden chambers of the psyche. These wounded places still cry out deep within us and must be allowed to come to consciousness and welcomed home.

NEVER ALONE

In the gospel, we read that Joseph had made up his mind to do something different when he was visited by an angel (cf. Mt 1:20). The experience moved him from hesitation to commitment. If you feel isolated on your journey, perhaps, especially in times of decision-making or expectancy, you can ask for an angel to bring you hope (and not just one of those cute little ornamental cherubs that are all 'in' at the moment!). Perhaps you can ask for a companion to be sent, in the way that Mary and Elizabeth, during their time of expectancy, were given in deep companionship and resonance with one another, 'from the moment your greeting reached my ear, the child leaped in my womb' (Lk 1:44).

Hope, in the words of Emily Dickinson, 'is the thing with feathers – that perches in the soul'. Having a hopeful heart does not mean we avoid, or are airlifted out of suffering, but it helps us to find a seed of possibility even amidst great difficulties. 'We are in difficulties on all sides but never cornered; we see no answer to our problems, but never despair; we have been persecuted but never deserted; knocked down but never killed'(2 Cor 4:8).

We have good reason to hope, even though we were never promised a perfect symphony here on this earth. Through the eyes of hope, we discover that life can be beautiful; while not perfect, it can be filled with meaning, even when laced with sorrow. Patience comes from the word 'patior' which means 'to suffer'. Just as the baby suffers when being thrust from the safety of the womb, we too suffer with the labour pains of being birthed and stretched from some old chrysalis into a new life.

Remember:

You are a precious jewel that cannot be tarnished, held in the hand of your Creator.

Over to You:

As you identify places of exile in yourself, perhaps you might find it helpful to pray into them using the following psalms: 42, 107, 127, 137.

Where and how have you been ordained to be a beacon of hope, bringing good news to those dark corners of the world? Is there anyone you know who needs a helping hand to raise them back to life? Will you be that hand?

Choosing Newness

Look I am doing something new, now it emerges, can
you not see it? Yes, I am making a road in the desert
and rivers in the wasteland. (Is 43:18)

One of the most difficult times to remain hopeful is
when we are grieving the loss of somebody that we
love. Unexpressed grief hardens and ossifies, becoming
'grievance'. To carry a grievance is a heavy weight on
the soul so we need to be able to grieve which helps to
irrigate us for new growth. We need to cry, howl and
wail for however long it takes. The time it takes cannot be
measured, controlled or harnessed.

However, after a period of time we often discover that,
though the physical structure of the relationship has gone
and our loved one is no longer visible to the eye, the essence
of what we shared lives on. When we release bitterness
about their parting, we discover that they, in many respects,
are still with us. All time is in the present so this eternal

moment contains all the love that united us and will continue to do so beyond this apparent ending.

Having to face our own mortality, as well as that of our loved ones, is probably the most important, if challenging, thing we must contend with on our earthly journey. While most sensible people aren't too enthused about the prospect of their own demise, keeping before us the inevitability of death helps us to live more fully in the now. More importantly, reflecting on death teaches us that we cannot ultimately call anybody or anything our final homeland, because we are *waiting in mindful hope* while journeying towards a larger belonging.

We endure many small deaths before our final death, perhaps none more distressing than the death of a relationship which we had cherished. Maybe it might help to remind ourselves that those who have 'left' us may become present again in some new way when we release them from any residual bitterness or blame. It may be heaven when we meet, or it may be next week, but in the meantime we can replace our talk about who was right and who was wrong, with sending blessings – even a small stingy blessing will be a start! It will do wonders for expanding our own hearts and providing a soothing balm for our own emotional heartburn.

KEEPING HOPE ALIVE

If we are to keep hope alive in our hearts, we have to train our minds to disengage from 'catastrophic thinking'. If we have been in a low mood for a long time, we tend to get so used to it that it can be difficult to rise to any new belief systems. However, through perseverance, we will eventually see the new little buds emerging in our consciousness.

Old habits die hard, we are told; old attitudes do not shift so easily, so we have to keep *doing* the new thing and the new belief until the feeling follows (and not the other way around). The path of least resistance is always a seductive one. It can often seem that the road that leads to life can be 'narrow' and at times a lonely one. However, we are assured that it is often the path that leads to our deepest joy (cf. Mt 7:13).

Embracing a spirit of 'newness' necessitates that we protect the embryonic new life against the many forces which act against it. In order to walk in newness, we may have to learn to say 'no', in order to embrace the new 'yes' in our lives. We have to protect our new freedom and 'not submit again to the yoke of slavery' (Rm 5:5).

We have to actively listen to more uplifting and life-giving news and no longer allow ourselves to become dominated and jaded by cynicism and doubt. We are, scripture advises, to 'keep watch' or our 'hearts will grow coarsened' (Lk

21:34). To prevent this coarsening of heart, we have to engender *new conversations, new attitudes and new decisions*. We have to shine our light from the hilltop for everyone to see, instead of allowing ourselves be like bushels dimming our own light. We have to go forward each day into the sunlight of the Holy Spirit, becoming a channel for the life flow of that Spirit.

MISSION IS POSSIBLE

Pope Francis tells us we have a mission to be hopeful:

> My Mission of being in the heart of the people is not just a part of my life or a badge I can take off; it is not an 'extra' or just another moment in life. Instead, it is something I cannot uproot from my being without destroying my very self. *I am a mission* on this earth; that is the reason why I am here in the world. We have to regard ourselves as sealed, even branded, by this mission of bringing light, blessing, enlivening, raising up, healing and freeing.

How does it feel to hear that, not only do you *have* a mission/purpose but you *are* a mission? Not only do you bring a blessing, but you *are* a blessing.

When we become messengers of hope and newness, we can be criticised and misunderstood; there will nearly always be one in the corner ready to throw cold water on us, one that says 'sure we tried that before and it didn't work', or 'sure it's too late now'. Like the prophets of old, we might have to withstand ridicule, especially when, in our zeal, we are considered to be a thorn in the side.

BELIEVE IT AND YOU WILL SEE IT

There is great comfort to be found in the affirmation that Habakkuk received from God in the Old Testament. It reminds us that in times of waiting, we must keep an eye on the vision/dream and to resolutely keep believing in it while we wait in mindful hope. It suggests that we write out our dream and then trust in its unfolding 'in its own time'.

> Write the vision down, inscribe it on tablets to be easily read, since this vision is for its own time only; eager for its own fulfilment, it does not deceive; if it comes slowly, wait, for come it will, without fail.
> (Habakkuk 2:2–3)

Remember:

We can actively watch for new buds emerging in our consciousness, when we notice signs of newness, we will begin to walk in newness.

Over to You:

Write out your own deepest hope/dream. Write it in pencil so that it can be erased and a new dream put in its place, so you remain open to any new inspiration as it becomes available.

If there is a situation that consistently drains your hope, begin to choose one of these responses: change the situation; change your response to the situation; leave the situation.

Joy

Pope Francis says: 'One of the more serious temptations which stifles boldness and zeal is a defeatism which turns us into querulous and disillusioned pessimists, 'sourpusses' (*Evangelii Gaudium*, 85). The sourpusses among us would need to heed a bit of his advice here, especially when hiding behind the guise of religion to justify those long faces! Joy, according to Pope Francis, is the great hallmark of those who have been touched by God's love; they become people 'who wish to share their joy, who point to a horizon of beauty and who invite others to a delicious banquet' (*Evangelii Gaudium*, 15).

A person who radiates joy becomes an infectious and luminous presence in the world, and is surely the best witness of the delicious banquet that Christ referred to as 'life to the full'. Know that your birthright is joy: 'I have said this so that my own joy may be in you and your joy is complete' (Jn 15:11). Notice the amount of times that joy is mentioned in the scriptures:

Go up on a high mountain, joyful messenger of Zion.
Shout with a loud voice. (Is 40:9)

The lord your God is in your midst, a victorious
warrior. He will exult with joy over you. (Zeph 3:17)

I want you to be happy, always happy in the Lord; I
repeat, what I want is your happiness. (Phil 4:14)

LOOKING TO THE STARS

Oscar Wilde said, 'We are all in the gutter but some of us
are looking at the stars.' It's all about what we choose to
look at, and *how we choose* to look at it. We see only 'gutter'
when we are focusing on what is lacking, or focusing on
what is wrong with us, but we see stars when we choose to
count our blessings, especially when we cultivate a spirit of
gratitude for everything and everyone around us. Through
overfamiliarity and habit, we often relate to others, not as
stars on our journey, but as useful 'props'. We greet others
with our checklists: did you put petrol in the car? Have you
paid the television licence? Did you pick up the milk? If,
however, we were to relate to them, as if it was their last
day on earth, we would *see them*, not through our list of
expectations, but for the shining stars that they really are.

When we no longer obstruct the view by our own self-obsession, we gain true access to the heart of another. Free of the interferences of our own filters, expectations and projections, we experience the joy of true encounter and connection.

To look towards the stars is an act of faith, it is a decision based on the belief that *if you believe it, you will see it* (and not the other way around). Joy is not about being permanently high, or having that fleeting 'don't worry be happy' feeling. The cultivation of joy calls for a rigorous and disciplined adherence to the values that bring meaning, calmness and purpose to both yourself and others. Looking to the stars means we no longer watch over our shoulder in the hope that some imagined bystander is being impressed by us. It means no longer longing for some illusory external applause to rescue us from our own self disapproval or self-loathing.

There is a left side of the brain called the anterior cingulate cortex. Activation of this is associated with the positive emotions we call joy. It is not activated through any external circumstances but through internal practices such as acceptance, gratitude and reflection.

A WILD AND JOYFUL GOD

The biblical poem known as 'The Song of Songs' includes a beautiful depiction of one who encounters us full of sensory joy, who calls us his 'lovely one' seeing us as beautiful, reassuring us that 'winter has gone, the flowers appear on the earth'. We can hold many conditioned resistances to what we might consider to be too 'wild' a God for us! If so, how about we allow ourselves to be shaken up a little by the God presented in the poem 'Tired of Speaking Sweetly' by the poet Hafiz.

Love wants to reach out and manhandle us,
Break all our teacup talk of God.

If you had the courage and
Could give the Beloved His choice, some nights,
He would just drag you around the room
By your hair,
Ripping from your grip all those toys in the world
That bring you no joy.

Love sometimes gets tired of speaking sweetly
And wants to rip to shreds
All your erroneous notions of truth
That make you fight within yourself, dear one,

And with others,

Causing the world to weep
On too many fine days.

God wants to manhandle us,
Lock us inside of a tiny room with Himself
And practice His dropkick.

The Beloved sometimes wants
To do us a great favor:

Hold us upside down
And shake all the nonsense out.

But when we hear
He is in such a 'playful drunken mood'
Most everyone I know
Quickly packs their bags
and hightails it
Out of town.

Who wouldn't try to 'hightail it' from a God who wants
to practise 'his dropkick' on us! We need to be very daring
to approach this unpredictable deity who might not agree

with the watered-down version of his message that many of us have embraced. The kingdom of God, it seems, belongs to the slightly mad ones: the poets, the mystics, those who the world consigns to the margins. You have to be a little 'out of your mind' to grasp God's 'playful drunken mood' because it is often the mind that bears the obstacles to our receiving the mystery. Maybe it is the child who will save us here, because apparently God is not usually revealed to the over-sensible or the 'wise and clever' (Lk 10:21). The cautionary, often manipulative, or cunning voices cannot hear with the same fresh intuition of the child. Playfulness and prayerfulness are not dissimilar; they both require a heart that can let go and trust. The child is the archetype of playfulness and can access the God who is 'for ever young and a constant source of newness' (*Evangelii Gaudium*, 11). It is interesting that God chose to come to earth as a child, as a little one, who at times must have had temper tantrums, a snotty nose and grazed knees.

When I was a child, my parents were frequently sick and often in hospital at Christmas. Sometimes Santa came a few days late, and one year, to my horror, he didn't come at all. I searched in vain on Christmas morning for what I hoped would be a parcel with the longed-for colouring book, slippers and selection box. I never forgave him, until Christmas morning thirty-five years later, when I woke to see a brightly coloured parcel at the end of the bed. I opened the old dusty card; it read:

Dear Martina,

I am so sorry that I didn't come that Christmas thirty-five years ago, but I want you to know that I never forgot you, and I've had these in my workshop all those years (the elves were looking for your address). I hope I got it right this time.

Love,

Santa

I opened the parcel and there was a little colouring book, a small pair of orange furry slippers (quite a few sizes too small!) and a selection box. My husband, Pat, was responsible for this gesture and it was a very healing experience. Somehow I don't think it was entirely a coincidence that I opened the card just hours before my mother died.

Strangely, even now, when I think of my mother's death, I also think of the Christmas that Santa visited! Moments of joy often sit alongside moments of sorrow; in fact, they come from the same place within us.

Even when there are seasons of drought in the terrain of the heart, we are to joyfully wait for the 'not yet' while fully attending to the now. We are to become less hijacked by internal mental dialogue and learn to respond rather than react to life events as they emerge. We must regularly return to the 'presence in the moment' each time our peace gets disturbed, until eventually this habit becomes as natural as breathing. We can remind ourselves that no moment, however exquisite or horrendous, is permanent, and so we begin again each day to trust in divine providence as life unfolds.

The winter tree, her long arms and gnarled fingers reaching up into the sky, stands dignified while she waits for her new buds. She asks us to stand beside her as we strengthen our trembling knees and raise our weary arms while *waiting in mindful hope*.

Remember:

If you believe it, you will see it!

Over to You:

Reflect on the following lines; maybe you could write them out on a sheet of paper and hang it somewhere as a reminder: wait patiently, walk deliberately and hope fiercely with your God.

Waiting in Mindful Hope

'Be-attitudes' for Waiting in Mindful Hope

Your life is a wonderful unfolding journey
In living fully in the here and now, you are born into the 'not yet'.
Do not run through your precious life, dismissing moments as being merely 'ordinary' or 'mundane'.
Slow down so that you may see where you have come from, and where you are going.
Go step by step, moment by moment, breath by breath, let silence do its work on you.
Inhale it all, treasure the gift, and do not pass it by in the quest for some grand finale.
Do not set goals according to society, or other people's expectations of you.
Listen to the small voice within; allow the drama of the mind to pass ...
You do not walk alone, so walk softly, patiently always Waiting in Mindful Hope.

Martina Lehane Sheehan

Ongoing Practice and Reflections

If you want to delve deeper in the practice of integrating everyday mindfulness, I recommend my double CD *Beyond Mindfulness: Guided Meditations and Soothing Lyrics*. The first CD will guide you through a morning, midday and evening meditation, while the second consists of soothing and reflective lyrics. It is available in Veritas shops and other retail outlets, online at veritasbooksonline.com or can be ordered at ruah06@eircom.net or martinalehanesheehan. com

If you want to learn more about integrating spirituality with mindfulness, you will find a psycho-spiritual approach alongside real life stories and practical steps in my bestselling titles *Seeing Anew: Awakening to life's Lessons* and *Whispers in the Stillness: Mindfulness and Spiritual Awakening*, both published by Veritas.